HOME OF HARD-TO-FIND BOOKS

Martin Hill's Charge; Or, the Forge and 'The Feathers' by F.W..
by F. W

Address:
HardPress
8345 NW 66TH ST #2561
MIAMI FL 33166-2626
USA
Email: info@hardpress.net

q ƒ 206

Page 25.

MARTIN HILL'S CHARGE;

OR,

THE FORGE AND "THE FEATHERS."

"Before the eyes of men let duly shine thy light,
But ever let thy life's best part be out of sight."

R. C. TRENCH.

PUBLISHED UNDER THE DIRECTION OF
THE COMMITTEE OF GENERAL LITERATURE AND EDUCATION,
APPOINTED BY THE SOCIETY FOR PROMOTING
CHRISTIAN KNOWLEDGE.

LONDON:

SOCIETY FOR PROMOTING CHRISTIAN KNOWLEDGE;
SOLD AT THE DEPOSITORIES:
77, GREAT QUEEN STREET, LINCOLN'S INN FIELDS;
4, ROYAL EXCHANGE; 48, PICCADILLY;
AND BY ALL BOOKSELLERS.

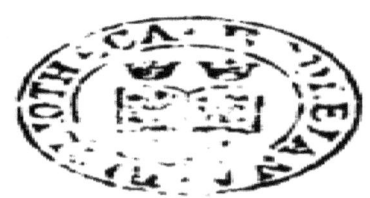

LONDON:

Printed by Truscott, Son, & Simmons,
Suffolk-lane City.

MARTIN HILL'S CHARGE;

OR,

THE FORGE AND "THE FEATHERS."

CHAPTER I.

THE FORGE.

"Under a spreading chestnut tree
 The village smithy stands.
 The smith, a mighty man is he,
 With large and pow'rful hands;
 And the sinews of his brawny arms
 Are strong as iron bands."

H. W. LONGFELLOW.

ONE of the short gloomy afternoons of early November was drawing to its close. The day had been fine for the time of year, but now the sky was dark with threatening clouds, the wind moaned dismally through the tree-tops, bringing down showers of the brown leaves that still remained, and the weather-

wise of Burnside predicted a stormy night.
It was just such an evening as would make
a man hasten back to his snug fireside, glad
to shut his door and draw in to the cosy
hearth: enjoying doubly the warmth and
comfort within, by contrast with the cheer-
less weather without.

But still there were two places, even in
little Burnside, which, on this evening, dull
as it was, kept many of the villagers from
their homes. Had you stopped on the hill,
looking down on the village, you might have
easily distinguished these by the bright spots
of light which indicated their situation.
One of these was the " Feathers," one of the
two inns of the village, standing just at the
bottom of the hill, a cheerful-looking place
enough in its way, with its gay sign-board
and brightly lighted parlour; but a sad
enemy to good Mr. Fearon, the rector, and
to many a thrifty housewife, and worst
enemy of all to many a thoughtless husband,
who sat there, evening after evening, drinking away his health, and wages, and good
character. The other point of attraction you

might easily discover, without the aid of
light, any time from seven in the morning
till four or five in the evening, by the
cheery music of the hammer and anvil, often
accompanied by the strong, tuneful notes of
the master of the village smithy. For those
steady ones of the place for whom the
"Feathers" had no charms, the forge, with
its blazing furnace, and Peter Barnet's kindly
face, formed often an evening meeting-place,
and to-night some topic of unusual interest
had gathered a larger number there than
usual.

The smithy might have formed a striking
picture that evening: without, the heavy
clouds and dreary wind; within, the group
of villagers in their rough, soiled, working
clothes, their tools slung across their shoul-
ders, gathered in the red glow of the fire
around the sturdy blacksmith—roughest and
swarthiest of all—his bare, muscular arms
crossed, leaning on his hammer, his head
raised, his face full of eagerness, his voice of
earnestness, as he talked to those around
him.

"Well, Mike Anderson," he was saying: "what I want to say is, that a finer young fellow than Martin Hill never breathed, and it'll be a bad day for Burnside when he leaves it, and that's what *I* think!" he concluded, bringing down the hammer with a thump on the anvil.

"I think you're about right there, Master Barnet," said a young man of about twenty. "It was a bad day for us youngsters when he left the school: it never was the same place afterwards. A steady, honest lad as he was, with no nonsense about him. And such a head piece, too! Why, many's the time I've heard Mr. Gilson say, that Mat Hill would turn out a great man some day. Ah, he *had* a headpiece for summing, and everything else, too, he had!"

"He didn't get that from his father," said the blacksmith; "an idle, drunken vagabond, as ever I saw. I never can bring myself, somehow, to speak to that man when I meet him, and, if I did, I should only get a surly answer for my pains."

"I'm sure it's a puzzle to me, how he

ever got such a son as Martin," remarked another.

"Oh, he was not always so," replied Barnet; "when he married, now near upon eight and twenty years ago, there wasn't a smarter lad in the place. And his wife, why there wasn't another young woman like her."

"Ah!" said a man who had been hitherto silent; "she was dead and buried before I knew Robert Hill, and I've often wondered what she was like. Precious different from the wife he's got now, I should think, to look at Martin."

"Different! I should think so. The prettiest, gentlest creature that ever lived. I believe it was she as kept her husband straight, and yet never said a harsh word to him in her life, I should think. But, bless you, I don't know who could have said her no, she had such a friendly sort of way with her, and Martin's just like her. Many a time I've thought to see his mother's own self looking out of those honest eyes of his."

"But whatever made him take up with Peg Scratchley?"

" Well, it do seem strange.   But you see
he was terrible cut up at poor Mary's death,
as well he might be.   But the trouble didn't
do him good, as it do some folks.   He never
was a man of much strength like—easily led
by those about him.   He got moped and
lonely, you see, and got going to the " Feathers" for company, and, maybe, because
there was nothing there to remind him of her
as he'd lost.   And then, you know, if a man
gets in that way, it needs a strong will to get
him out of it again, and that he never had.
Then he took up with Peg Scratchley, and
things got from bad to worse ; and how they
are ever to mend, now Martin's going, I'm
sure I don't know."

" But what made him marry again?"

" What makes a moth fly into a candle?
You may as well ask one as the other.   But
there, there's many a fool as 'll go to ruin for
a pretty face and a smart bonnet ; and Peg
could look spruce enough when she pleased.
But here's Martin himself coming down the
road."

Peter Barnet was right, and in another

minute Martin Hill had joined the group of
men. Though scarcely twenty-seven, you
might easily have added ten years to his age,
so early had thought and care marked the
otherwise handsome young face. But, not-
withstanding this, there was enough in the
great earnest blue eyes, in the sunny smile
that lit up his face when pleased, and in the
whole bearing of his tall, strongly built
figure, to show that no trouble had been
great enough to sour a naturally sweet temper, or mar his enjoyment of the innocent
pleasures of life. Martin Hill's was a
strange history. He had known his first
sorrow in the death of his mother, when he
was twelve years old, followed, within a year,
by his father's second marriage to a wife
with disposition utterly opposed to that of
her predecessor. Martin had been sent
early to school by his careful mother, and
had there shown a taste for learning quite
unusual at his age. His rapid progress soon
attracted the notice of the clergyman, Mr.
Fearon, who became much interested in the
clever, thoughtful young scholar. On his

mother's death he was removed by his kind patron from the village school to one of a higher character, and from thence to a training college for schoolmasters, as he had expressed a strong wish for this vocation, for which his unusual genius seemed admirably to fit him. A short time before my story opens, an Australian clergyman had written to this college, offering a first-rate opening for a young man of moderate experience in teaching, as master of a newly-built school in his parish. This had been offered to Hill, who, after some hesitation, accepted it, though not without much regret at leaving his home and friends.

With his father, meanwhile, as we have already heard, things had been getting from bad to worse. His second wife proved to be a wasteful, careless manager, a violent tempered, undutiful wife, and a negligent, almost cruel mother. She had several children, but all died, save one little boy. Sad, indeed, was the contrast between the childhood of Robert Hill's two sons: little Martin always clean, rosy, happy, a very pattern of what a mother's care and love can do; setting off morning by morning for the village school; returning every evening to his bright happy home, to a cozy half-hour before bedtime, sitting on his little stool beside mother's knee, whilst father smoked his pipe and listened, well pleased to listen to his boy's talk of all his doings at school. Then there was Sunday, the happiest day of all, when father's tools were laid aside, and mother's best bonnet and gown were put on, and they went to church together, with their little son trotting between them. Martin had always been taught to regard church as a great pleasure, and it was a pretty sight to see the little fair-haired lad sitting so still beside his mother, with his blue eyes fixed so earnestly on the clergyman, as if he were straining all his childish powers to understand the holy prayers and lessons that he heard.

Such was Martin's childhood; but with little Robert, or Robin (as he was called), ah, how different! A wretched home, an idle, drunken father, a neglectful, scolding mother; always dirty and ragged, spending his

life, Sundays and week-days alike, loitering
about the streets with all the idle, good-for-
nothing boys of the village. Little, indeed,
is it to be wondered at, if the two boys grew
up very different. But we have been wandering too long from our story, and while we
have done so the forge has been left empty
of its occupants, save Martin Hill and Peter
Barnet.

"Now we are alone," said Martin, as the
last of the group left the smithy, "I have
something to speak to you of: something I
want you to do for me. Maybe it's the last
favour I shall ever ask of you, old friend, so
I hope you'll grant it me."

"Not the last, I hope, Martin. I'm not
so young as I was, it's true; but I'm hale
and hearty yet, and, please God, I have
many a horse to shoe, and many a nail to
drive, before I lay down the old hammer for
good. And as for you, my lad, why, in a
year or two you'll be coming back a great
man, looking down on us poor folks at
home."

"Never that!" said Martin, smiling;

"and I hope, as you say, we shall both be spared for many a long day. But what I wanted to talk to you about, was that young brother of mine. I can't bear the thought of leaving him, as it were, without a friend in the world to look after him;" and Martin sighed deeply as he thought of the neglect of those parents, who should have been the boy's best friends. After a pause, he continued: "I've been doing all I can to put him in the right way, these few weeks I've been at home, and I think he'd like to be steady if he could, poor boy : but I don't know how it'll be when I'm gone. So I thought I'd ask you to do what you can for the child—*your* child and mine, too, in one sense, Peter. You remember the day we both promised for him before God ? "

"Ah ! that I do ! " said Barnet, gravely; and, in the silence that followed, the thoughts of both travelled back to a certain Sunday, ten years ago, when a burly, rough-faced man of thirty-five, and a tall, slender stripling of seventeen, had stood together beside the font in the old village church, and promised that

a rosy, chubby little lad of three should re-
nounce the world, the flesh, and the devil,
and, keeping God's holy will and command-
ments, should walk in the same until his
life's end.   Martin was then just going to
leave his native village for London, and had,
after some difficulty, obtained his desire that
little Robin should be baptized: a duty which
Mrs. Hill regarded as "a pack of rubbish,"
and her husband was too indolent to care
about.

Upon this scene, ten years after, the two
sponsors looked back for a while, before
they looked onward again to the dark, un-
certain future.

"Martin," said the blacksmith," at last,
very gravely; "it's a solemn thing to promise so much for a child, and I fear I've not
done what I should by him.   But, somehow,
I can't bear poking myself into other people's
matters; and if I did, why there, Mat, I never
had it in me, like you, to make the youngsters take to me.   I'm too rough and
awkward with them, somehow.   Now, with
you it seems as if you had only to whistle, to

have all the little ones in this place at your heels."

"Yes, it seems so," said Martin, laughing; "though I don't know why it should be. But I'm sure you could make Robin fond of you, if you chose, for he's a good little chap at the bottom; and, O master," continued the young man, eagerly, "if I could but think he had you as a friend to look to, it would take such a weight off my mind."

"Then you may think so," said Barnet, earnestly, grasping his friend's hand warmly, in token of his sincerity. "I'll do my best for the lad, for your sake. I don't see my way clear to it now, but, please God, I shall soon."

"You can always pray for him, Peter, and for me when I'm far away, and for poor father, too, as I shall do for you all."

"That I will, indeed," said Barnet, and tears stood in his eyes as he spoke. "I will both pray and work too, till we meet again."

"Till we meet again!" echoed Martin; and often, afterwards, those words came back

to the blacksmith's mind with a strange
thrill.   When should that meeting be?

> " Never here, for ever there
> Where all parting, pain, and care,
> And death, and time, shall disappear
> For ever there, and never here ! "

CHAPTER II.

MORNING WORK.

" Live I, so live I
  To my Lord heartily,
  To my Prince faithfully,
  To my neighbour honestly,
  Die I, so die I."

H. W. LONGFELLOW.

THE first streaks of dawn had but just shown
themselves in the dark east; yet, early as was
the hour, Peter Barnet was astir and working
hard. It was a frosty morning, and soon the
footsteps were heard on the hard white road
of two persons advancing at a brisk pace.

It was too dark to distinguish them easily,
but Peter had evidently been expecting them,
for he laid down his hammer, and, going to
the door, exclaimed, " You're a bit late,
Martin—leastways by the church clock. I'm
up betimes, you see, for I was determined to
have a last look at you on your way to the
station."

"Just like you, Peter; and indeed, there's no one in the place I'd rather see the last thing than you, unless it be Cock Robin here, who is pretty nearly exhausted with trying to keep up with me. I've been telling him, Peter, that you and I have been great friends, and that he must be your friend in my place, when I'm gone—eh, Robin?"

The boy looked shyly up at Peter from under his long eyelashes, as if he was not quite sure that he liked the arrangement; indeed, as he himself had said, the blacksmith was by no means a general favourite with the village boys, for he was a solitary man, and very reserved, and wont to speak somewhat too bluntly to please the children, so that hitherto Robin had kept out of his way.

Peter, on his side, looked at the boy almost as shyly himself, scarcely knowing what to say; and Martin continued,—

"I must not stay here any longer, though. So good-bye, my dear old friend; and God bless you, and grant we may meet again; if not here, at least in a better world than this."

Barnet could not speak, but he squeezed his friend's hand silently; then, as Martin was turning away, he called suddenly to Robin, "Here, my lad: you can just step in here on your way back—I want you to do a job for me before school." Then he turned to his work, and hammered away as if his life depended on it.

After a while he stopped, muttering his thoughts half-aloud, as was his way when anything puzzled him. "I don't know what good I've done by it now; however, it's a beginning, and no harm's done, anyhow. There never was such a blunderer as I am with children. I suppose I ought to talk religious, and give good advice, and all that; but there—I can't. I ain't no parson, nor ever shall be."

So he went on mumbling and hammering by turns, and puzzling his head sorely over Martin's parting charge to him. Barnet, besides being (as I have said) a very shy man, and especially so with children, had an almost overstrained horror of what he called "cant." He was one of those who

love to serve God best in silence, and their
neighbour by simple kindness, and by the
example of an honest, upright life; one of
those "holy and humble men of heart" who
shrink from teaching and advising others,
feeling their own ignorance and weakness;
and so now, when the post of guide and
teacher seemed almost thrust upon him,
it puzzled him sorely to see the way of
his duty.   But yet, though he knew it not,
Peter Barnet, the sensitive, reticent man, was
the one of all others best fitted to win little
Robin to the ways of right.   From his ear-
liest childhood Robin had learnt to despise
and mock at "cant," though in a widely different sense of the word to Peter Barnet's;
for with Mrs. Hill "cant" meant the same as
religion, and I need scarcely say that this
was not what the blacksmith meant by it.
"None of your rubbishing church stuff for
me!" Mrs. Hill would say.   "Martin may
go and make a parson of himself if he likes,
as long as he keeps out of *my* way, but my
boy shall never be so.   'Fine words butter
no parsnips,' I say, nor religious stuff neither.

Bob shall grow up a plain man, neither better nor worse than his neighbours." Such was the only moral teaching given by the mother to her son, when, indeed, she took the trouble to teach him at all. So Robin learned to call religion "cant," and to consider Martin, much as he loved him, as "a bit of a Methodist." Our story will show whether, in such a case, much talk on religious subjects is needful to influence for good, or whether simple Christian kindness, and the brightness of a good example, will do the work which our Great Example intended when He said, "Let your light so shine before men, that they may *see* your good works, and glorify your Father which is in Heaven."

Peter worked on steadily for half-an-hour, and then began to pause and listen, looking occasionally up the road, and murmuring, "Will he come, now, I wonder? I dare say not—most likely not, I'll warrant. Perhaps I shouldn't have spoke so rough, but it's always the way with me. Never mind— better luck next time!"

But Peter was wrong. Within another

half-hour Robin Hill had slunk into the smithy, and stood silently before the black-smith, watching him with an expression partly frightened, partly sullen, partly de-fiant. The two formed a curious sight : the big, rough blacksmith, eyeing his little charge with a troubled, anxious face, scratching his head in sore perplexity, alto-gether terribly ill at ease in his new position; the little shabby, neglected boy, gazing at Peter with keen, bright eyes, more than half-inclined to turn and bolt out of the door, and cut the business altogether. He did not do so, however, for Martin's last words still rang in his ears :

" Be a good lad, Cock Robin. Do what Master Barnet bids you, and don't forget your old brother when he's gone."

" Gone ! " And as he stood there, and thought of it, a great choking sob rose in Robin's throat, and his eyes grew dim, and the pent-up sorrow came bursting up from the poor little forlorn heart. The hot tears seemed all at once to melt the ice that had frozen Peter's tongue to silence.

"What! crying, old man? Come, that'll never do. It's only babies that cry, you know; and you'd best look sharp, or you'll put my fire out. That's right—choke them down like a man! Now, then, just work them bellows till I tell you to stop, and then we'll see what your arms are made of."

Robin obeyed the order readily. The words were rough, it is true, but there was something in Peter's voice—a ring of the true metal of kindness—that cheered the boy wonderfully; something, too, perhaps, had roused his pride a little, for he remarked, after working in silence for some minutes—

"I ain't a baby, master."

"Ain't you? Well, I'm glad to hear it. I suppose it must have been some one else I heard blubbering just now."

Robin looked puzzled, coloured a little, and then laughed, as he saw a sly twinkle in the blacksmith's eye.

"You're quizzing me!"

"Well, suppose I am. Now, look out, youngster; what are you letting the fire down for?—I didn't tell you to stop, did I?

That'll do" (when Robin had worked on a
little longer). "Now, I wonder if you can
take that bar out of the fire. There's a man!
you're stronger than I thought for. Now,
take the hammer yonder, and see which of
us can hit the hardest."

Robin obeyed all these directions with
alacrity. The cheery fire and the exertion
had warmed his cold fingers, and brought a
colour to his white cheeks, and his eyes were
bright with interest in the new employment.
Real occupation, indeed, of any kind, was a
novelty to the boy. With the exception of
the last few weeks before his brother's departure, he had lived in almost total idleness;
and when, through Martin's persuasion, he
had been sent to school, the master had
found him so ignorant that he was placed at
the bottom of the school, among those far
younger than himself, where he had little
encouragement to industry. But now,
working, working like a man—real hard
work, too—there was something very dig-
nified in it, and Robin felt quite an important
person, and realised, for the first time in his

life, the satisfaction of being useful. So, when the church clock struck a quarter to nine, and Peter Barnet sent him off to school, Robin trudged off, highly pleased with his labours, and full of pleasure, as he readily promised to be at the forge the following morning. As for the blacksmith, if not so proud as Robin, he certainly was not dissatisfied with the morning's work, at least if one might judge by the smile that lingered on his face as he watched the boy running down the hill. Then, as he turned and saw Robin's hammer lying in a corner, the smile expanded to a grin, and Master Barnet laughed to himself at the recollection of his young pupil's first essay at smith's work.

"Poor old anvil!" he said, chuckling to himself; "I fancy you and the crowbar shared the blows pretty equally between you. I warrant I should get but a poor living, if the iron got only ten out of every score of blows, in Master Robin's fashion. But, however that may be, the job this morning hasn't done me nor my anvil much harm; nor, please God, the young chap neither."

CHAPTER III.

WORK AND WAGES.

"Build to-day, then, strong and sure,
  With a firm and ample base;
  And, ascending and secure,
  Shall to-morrow find its place."

H. W. LONGFELLOW.

ROBIN HILL continued his morning visits to
the forge very regularly. He did not, it is
true, do much real work, certainly not as
much as he himself fancied he did; but the
blacksmith did not mind this, for, in truth,
he was delighted with the success of his simple experiment, and at the growing intimacy
which existed between himself and his young
charge. Not that they were either of them
very talkative. Sometimes the hour would
pass almost in total silence, broken only by
Peter's blunt orders, or, occasionally, even
by a sharp rebuke to his pupil for some
blunder in his work. "Now, then, butter-
fingers, what are you after? the hammer

won't bite you!" or, "Look sharp there,
youngster: you're a fine workman, I must
say!" or, "What are you gaping out of the
door for? an idle young rascal, as ever I
saw!" &c. &c.

But Robin never cared for these occasional rough words, for he was well used to
rough, or even cruel ones, at home; and he
even liked them sometimes, "Just to show I
ain't a baby, as he thought me at first, and
don't mind a cuff now and then." They
never did him any harm, I think, but rather
good (as rough words do, occasionally, when
not used needlessly) by stirring up the boy to
fresh exertion, and reminding him of the
importance of being careful in the smallest
details of his work.

Sometimes, however, they would talk a
little, and Barnet often got much amusement
from the boy's sharp remarks. Martin was
a frequent topic of conversation, and the
blacksmith was quite pleased to tell of the
days when he was a little child, and how he
used to like to come to the forge and watch
the bright sparks fly, and listen to the roar

of the furnace. Sometimes, Robin would talk of school—his lessons, friends, pleasures, and troubles there, and he soon found that he had not only a very patient but also a very sympathetic listener, ready to laugh heartily over some schoolboy prank, or lend his wits to unravel the difficulties of a hard lesson.

One Monday morning, Robin came into the smithy with a bright face. "I needn't go away so soon to-day, master. I can stop all day, if you like, and to-morrow and next day too, and every day!"

"What! holidays begun already?" asked Peter, in surprise.

"No, it isn't that; but I can't go to school any more now. Mother won't let me."

"Won't she? why not? I should have thought she would have been glad to be quit of an idle young vagabond like you, hanging about the place all day."

"I don't know. She says she has no money to throw away; and it don't matter now Martin's away, and no one left to worrit her to death about it. That's what mother said; and I ain't sorry neither, for I do hate them sums, and spelling, and things. I'd a deal sooner work along with you, master!"

Barnet was silent, and his face grew very grave as Robin spoke. Here was the first difficulty he had met with. It would never do to leave school now, and, especially, for a boy like Robin, who needed strict discipline to bring him to order and to counteract the evil influences of his bad home. But what was to be done? he knew well that it would be useless to remonstrate with Mrs. Hill, or else, much as he would naturally have shrunk from it, he would have done so; and as to her husband, Peter was well aware that, even if he were open to conviction, his passive approval would be of no avail without that of his more resolute and determined wife. There seemed but one alternative, to pay the weekly twopence himself, and this Peter could but ill afford; and besides, it would not do to let Robin become in any way dependent on him, when he had parents who were really able, and whose duty it was, to support him. So the blacksmith worked on

for some time in perplexed silence, turning the difficulty over and over in his mind. All at once he raised his head and asked,—
" What's the time, Rob?"

" Near upon eight, sir.",

" Well, look here, youngster. You say your mother won't pay your schooling, and I'm not going to neither. So what then?"

" Well, I suppose I can't go."

" And be a dunce all your life. How will you like that?"

" I don't like my book."

" More shame to you, then. But I didn't ask you if you liked your book, but if you wished to be a dunce."

Robin hung his head, and his eyes filled with tears as he replied, in a low voice, "No, I don't want to be a dunce; but it seems I can't help it."

" Why can't you?"

" Why, because no one will pay for me."

" Then you must pay for yourself."

Robin stared, in great amazement—" I can't get no money, sir!"

" Well, would you go if you had some?"

"Yes, I would; but I don't see how I'm to get any. I want to learn, I think."

"There's a man. You won't be a dunce no more than a baby, eh? Well, now, look here. School is at nine. If you come here by seven every day, and work hard, I'll give you twopence a week, and that'll take you to school. But mind you, I ain't going to *give* you the money. You must earn it for yourself; and if you miss coming one day, I shan't pay you anything for the week. What do you say? Will you come?"

Robin's eyes brightened with pleasure. Not only work but wages! To pay for his own schooling, and not to have to ask anybody! This was grand, indeed.

"Won't I come!" he exclaimed; "I should think so indeed, and thank you for it, master!"

"Don't thank me, youngster. I tell you I shan't pay you for nothing: you must work hard."

"See if I don't! may I begin to-day?"

"Well, you can if you like, I suppose; but you weren't here till half-past seven, and we have been wasting half the time talking, so you must come earlier to-morrow, to make up for lost time."

"All right, sir."

Then master and pupil worked very hard till a quarter to nine, almost in silence; and Robin trudged off to school, feeling at least two inches taller, and with two firm determinations in his mind:—First, That no one should ever call him a dunce again; and, second, That he would be worth his weekly twopence to his master.

CHAPTER IV.

THE "FEATHERS."

"Stay at the third glass, or forego the place.
Drink, above all things, doth God's stamp deface."
GEORGE HERBERT.

"ROME was not built in a day!" is a true proverb in many cases; and, among others, in that of Robin Hill's education.

Had the care of him been entirely committed to the good blacksmith, a few months might have wrought a considerable change in him; good habits might have been formed, bad ones got rid of, and the example of a good man's simple daily life might have done its work. Even as it was, Robin was learning more than either he or his master were at all aware of—learning habits of industry, to love honest work, to be manly and self-reliant, and, above all, to wish to imitate the habits of an upright, God-fearing man. Perhaps some of my readers will say that,

in all his efforts for Robin's good, Peter
Barnet was utterly neglecting the first duty,
"the one thing needful;" teaching him to
be busy and careful in earthly matters, whilst
the *real* business of life, "Our Father's business," was forgotten.   Most likely, had you
said so to the blacksmith, he would have
acknowledged the justice of your words, for,
indeed, these very same doubts and fears
were constantly in his mind.   But he knew
not how to begin, though he daily prayed
earnestly for help and guidance; and yet I
think, that though he did not know it, help
and guidance *were* given him, and that he
was in his turn helping and guiding his little
charge in the right way.   We must do all
things by degrees, "precept upon precept,
line upon line."   The little child must learn
first to look up into its father's face for help
and strength, before it can look onwards,
upwards, to its other dearer Father.   We
cannot love God all at once.   We must all
learn (as little Robin was learning) to love
justice, uprightness, truth, before we can
truly love the Truth Himself; to love the

Author through His works, the Giver through His wonderful gifts.

But, reader, you must not think from this that two hours daily spent in hard work with an honest man was enough to make Robin Hill a good boy. Before jumping to so sadly wrong a conclusion, we must look a little at his home life, which, as you will presently say, seemed more than enough to undo all the good the blacksmith could do him. Matters in the Hill household seemed to grow daily worse. The husband became more and more enslaved to his besetting sin. His health was gone, his mind fast going. Soon the more respectable farmers refused to take so untrustworthy a servant, and often weeks would pass away in helpless idleness. "And even," as his wife remarked, "when work did come the money did not come with it;" for day by day his wages were left at the "Feathers," in exchange for the misery and discord which were brought home instead of them.

Not that (even putting his father out of the question) Robin's home was one of peace

and comfort.   Mrs. Hill, as I have said before, was a woman in no way fitted to bring
these blessings to her household.   Violent
tempered, idle, and disorderly, she passed
most of her time wandering from house to
house, gossiping about other people's business, and spreading evil reports, slander, and
ill-will, wherever she went.   Many people
said that the wrong was chiefly on the wife's
side, and that the husband could not be
blamed for spending his evenings at the
" Feathers," when he had only a miserable
home and a scolding wife to come back to.
But I think that the evil was pretty equally
divided, and the result of it was, that when
the husband and wife did meet, their house
was, usually, a scene of bitter strife, violent
language, and even blows, till Robin often
escaped, frightened, from the place, to
wander half the night about the lanes and
fields, making his bed under a rick or some
empty shed.   He was not now, however,
even so well off as this always.   In an unlucky moment he had told his mother the
conditions on which he obtained his school-

ing, and this became a fresh and constant source of dispute between his parents. Mrs. Hill declared that her boy should never be going to "that stuck-up Methodist, old Sledgehammers, to be made a parson of like Martin," or to the school, "to have his head stuffed with nonsense, of no use to anybody." Whilst her husband retorted (partly out of opposition to his wife, and partly, perhaps, from a lingering feeling that it might not, after all, be such a bad thing if Robin were to grow up in Martin's fashion) that he wouldn't have the boy interfered with by any one, and he might go to school, or anywhere else he chose, as long as he didn't have to pay." Then Robin would be dragged into the quarrel, and very sad it was to hear the child siding with father against mother, and raising his young voice in taunts and bitter sneers.

A dispute of this kind had arisen one Sunday afternoon, in consequence of Robin's having refused to run an errand for his mother on the following day, on the ground of having to go to school, accompanying his refusal with as much impudence as he could think of, much to the amusement of his father, who sat in the door, smoking, and spelling out an article from a dirty sporting newspaper.

"That's the way; go it, youngster! never be tied to an old woman's apron-string," he said, with a loud laugh, in which Robin joined, which procured him a sound box on the ear.

"How dare you speak in that way?" said Mrs. Hill, crimson with passion. "You young rascal! you won't go to Skilston, won't you? But you shall, though, for all your impertinence. What's that you are mumbling about, Hill?" she added, turning on her husband, who had risen from his seat.

"What's that to you?" he retorted, sulkily; "not as I'm going to bide here, if you begin your noise again. I'm off to the 'Feathers,' so you may scold yourself hoarse if you choose, so long as I'm out of the way. Come on, Bob: you'd best come along with me, I think."

"Aye, get out of the house with you, do!"

screamed his angry wife, as Hill moved
away. " And you, too, Robin : go and follow
your brute of a father, and I don't care if I
never set eyes on you again."

Robin heard no more, for he had followed
his father, glad to escape the storm of abuse
which followed him. So the two passed on
through the quiet village, where the church
bells were ringing for evening service, down
the hill to the noisy " Feathers," where the
day and the day's Lord seemed alike shut
out.

I will not attempt a minute description of
how that evening was passed. Robin had
but a vague, confused remembrance afterwards of a close room, from which the pure
evening air and light were excluded, and in
their place flaring gas lamps and the fumes
of spirits and tobacco. He recollected creep-
ing at first behind his father's chair, listening,
half puzzled, half amused, to the ribald songs
and jests of those around him. Then some
one had called for the young chap to sing a
song, and his father had pulled him forward
and put a glass of something hot and strong

to his lips, bidding him "take a drop to find his voice, and sing out like a man, the first that came into his head." After this his remembrances became still more hazy. He could but dimly remember singing, as bidden, the first thing that came into his head, a hymn he had learnt at school, encouraged by the roars of laughter of his father and his dissolute comrades. And then the hostess of the "Feathers," a stout, red-faced woman, with a loud voice, patted him on the back and called him "a fine little man," and gave him some more hot stuff, only much sweeter than his father's. After this, Robin recollected no more till a wretched awaking, to find himself nearly in the middle of next day, with a torturing headache and a confused feeling of utter helplessness, both of mind and body. For some time he lay there, wondering how he got home the night before, and why he felt so ill. Then he remembered that he had missed his work at the forge and his school too, and wondered what Master Barnet would say, and whether he would really keep back his wages as he had said. At all events, he would not go there to-day, he felt too ill; and, somehow, he could not bear the thought of meeting the blacksmith's keen eyes. So he spent most of the day tossing restlessly about on his bed, with occasional snatches of troubled sleep, disturbed by terrible dreams. Towards the afternoon he crawled down-stairs, but soon returned, glad to get out of the way of his mother's sharp, grating voice, which seemed to go through his aching head like a knife.

Tuesday morning found Peter Barnet hard at work, as usual, when a miserable little figure, with white cheeks and heavy eyes, crept into the smithy and stood before him. The blacksmith eyed him, narrowly, from head to foot, and then remarked, drily, "You don't seem quite up to the mark to-day, youngster."

"Oh, I'm all right," said the boy, huskily; "I wasn't here yesterday, master."

"You needn't have told me that, I should think. Were you ill?"

"No," in a very low voice.

"What, lazy? Well, it's a pity, I think.

An hour in bed isn't worth a week's schooling, to my mind. But you know best what suits you."

Robin thought that the hour in bed had not suited him at all; and, also, was a good deal disappointed to find that his master intended to carry out his intention with regard to work and wages, so he only muttered, sulkily, "Then I can't go to school, if you won't give me the money."

"Of course you can't. I told you before what would happen, if you shirked work."

"I didn't think you meant it."

"Didn't mean it? Now, look here, my lad: just remember, I *always* mean what I say."

"Then, I suppose, I mustn't work," said Robin, after a pause.

"That's as you like."

"Should I be any use?"

"Of course you would. I shouldn't pay you if you were not."

Robin took up the hammer with a feeling of relief, but he soon found that the traces of his evening at the "Feathers" had by no means disappeared. His hand shook so that he could scarcely hold the hammer, and his blows were weak and unsteady, often entirely missing their mark. The motion, too, made him giddy, and everything seemed to dance before his eyes.

Peter watched him steadily for a minute, and then asked, "Where have you been to, Robin? Tell me the truth."

Robin's cheek was crimson now, and he quailed before the blacksmith's stern glance.

"Come! out with the truth, my boy."

"At the 'Feathers,' sir."

Peter gave a long, low whistle. "And that is what has made you ill, is it?"

"I suppose so, sir."

An expression of pain passed across the master's rough face. Then he said, quite quietly, "Lay down the hammer, young fellow; I must work alone, though I'm sorry for it."

"O sir! why mayn't I work?"

"Look here, boy: Forge and 'Feathers' can't go together; they never have yet, and never shall. You must stick to one or the

other—the choice is your own." Then he
stopped, and went on muttering to himself,
" No man can serve two masters. Either he
will love the one and hate the other, or else
he will cleave to the one and despise the
other."

Robin listened to these words with droop-
ing head, thoroughly frightened and abashed.
He had never before seen his master angry,
and his anger terrified him. He was so quiet,
yet so in earnest, using no threats or violent
words, scarcely raising his voice above its
usual pitch; and yet there was something in
his manner that made the boy tremble—a
tone of mingled indignation, sorrow, and
pity, very different from the brutal rage of
his father, or the passionate outbursts of his
mother. He stood silent and confounded,
not knowing what to answer.

" I'm very sorry, sir," he said at last, half
sobbing; " I won't go to the ' Feathers' any
more."

" Don't promise in a hurry," was the short
answer; and Robin was turning away dis-
couraged, when Peter's hand was laid on his

arm, and he said, very gently, looking down kindly into the little woe-begone face, "What makes you sorry, Cock Robin?"

It was Martin's old pet name, and the boy fairly broke down. "O sir, I can't bear to make you angry! there's no one else so kind to me. O sir, won't you ever take me back? I don't want to go to the 'Feathers' again, indeed I don't!"

"Well, there, don't cry, old chap; I didn't mean to be hard on you, for we all of us makes blunders sometimes, I suppose. I can't go back from what I said about the work and the pay this week, and if I did you ain't fit for it to-day; so you'd best go home, only mind you keep out of mischief."

Robin left the forge considerably comforted, though still rather downcast, turning over in his mind all that Peter had said. What his meditations were we will not pause to consider. Suffice it to say, that he kept his word, and did not again visit the "Feathers."

CHAPTER V.

BAD TIDINGS.

"——— If we could but see
 The joy in angels' eyes
 O'er good lives and heroic deaths
 Of pure self-sacrifice,
 We should not weep o'er those that sleep,
 Their short, sharp struggle o'er,
 Under the rolling waves that break
 Upon the distant shore."

D. M. MULOCH.

TILL we meet again! With what a strange, new, solemn meaning, did those parting words of Martin Hill's come back to Peter Barnet, when he knew that the voice which had spoken them was silent for ever on earth—that they should never meet again till they met never more to part in heaven. "I will both pray and work for Robin till we meet," had been his promise to Martin; and now it stood, "I will pray and work for him till death, his death or mine."

The sad news came to the blacksmith early one Sunday morning, about three weeks after Robin's unhappy visit to the "Feathers." A friend had sent him a newspaper containing the account of the "Loss of the Steamship Albert, off Melbourne." Then followed the touching tale of the brave ship going down in sight of land; of desperate efforts made to save some few lives; of nearly a hundred souls launched suddenly into the great ocean of eternity. Near the end came a passage, read and re-read many times in Burnside:—"Amidst the terror and confusion that reigned among the unfortunate passengers, a clergyman, the Rev. Mr. B—, and a young man named Hill, did much, by their noble example and encouraging words, to restore order and resignation; indeed, it is mainly to their efforts that those few who have been saved, owe their escape, We are sorry to have to add that neither of these gentlemen were among the survivors."

"Gentlemen! Aye, Martin was a gentleman, if ever one lived," murmured Barnet to himself, as he laid down the paper which his eyes had grown too dim to read: "Yes, it was just his own brave self, thinking of every one before himself."

"I wish to God he had never gone!" said the neighbour who brought the news.

"No," said the blacksmith, gravely; "we'd better say, rather, bless the Lord for sending our Martin to help and comfort the poor souls in their trouble. Who can say, but many a soul without him might have gone to meet his God all unprepared."

Then, as the neighbour left him, Peter opened his Bible and read of Him who stilled the raging waves; and of the land where there is no more sea, where he and Martin might some day meet again. So he read on till the thought of Robin and his unhappy parents flashed into his mind. "Their trouble is greater than mine," he said, rising. "Maybe, I can be of some help to the poor folks in their affliction." So he went down to the Hills' cottage, feeling himself no welcome visitor, yet hoping to find a way to be of use.

Sad, indeed, was the scene in the bereaved

household; though, perhaps, in some respects
not so really sad as usual, for a common
sorrow had, for once, united the husband
and wife. Through all his neglect and
intemperance Robert Hill had been very
proud of his clever, prosperous son, and
his wife, little as she had cared for him,
had still a sort of despairing conviction,
that with him the last hope of respectability
for the family was gone. Both, too, had
half unconsciously looked forward, with that
helpless belief in the future so often to be
found in those leading sinful lives, to a good
time that was to come, when Martin would
return a rich man and raise them all to comfort and decency again. But now the blow
had fallen, and both seemed, for a time,
utterly overwhelmed by it.

Mrs. Hill opened the door to Peter Barnet's knock, and when she saw who it was she
covered her face with her apron and, throw-
ing herself into a chair, sobbed aloud. The
unhappy husband sat on a chair by the fire,
his face buried in his hands, and did not raise
it till Peter touched him on the shoulder.

Then he started away from him, saying, almost savagely, "What do you want here? we never were friends; so why do you come here now, when no one wants you? I suppose you want to mock at us now we're down."

"No," said Peter, gently; "I couldn't well have come for that, being down myself. Come, neighbour: if we haven't been on the best of terms before, let us be friends now, when we are both in such sore trouble."

"What's my boy's death to you? He wasn't your son."

"No; but he was my best friend on earth. He was as dear to me as a son."

"What are you here for?"

"To see if I can help you."

"Help! What help can you be? There's no one who can comfort me."

"You're right there, Master Hill, there is no one who can comfort you, at least not on earth ——"

"Begone, will you?" cried Hill, starting up angrily. "I don't want any of your preaching here, I say; leave me alone."

Barnet saw that words were useless, so he turned and looked for Robin. "Where's the boy?" he asked of Mrs. Hill; and, following the motion of her hand, groped his way up the dark narrow staircase. The boy had flung himself down on the bare boards under the window of the small, comfortless bedroom, and in that position had sobbed himself to sleep. Now he lay slumbering peacefully, a faint ray of winter sunlight stealing in through the casement across his pale, tear-stained face, and resting softly among the matted curls of his dark hair. Robin had never been a pretty child; but now, as Peter stood looking down on him, there was a gentle, sorrowful look in the sleeping face that he had never seen there before, that reminded him strongly of Martin. Presently the sleeper stirred, and opening his great, sad, dark eyes, gazed wonderingly at his visitor. Then he smiled with pleasure as he recognised him, and asked, "Is that *you* here, master?"

"Yes, my poor old chap, it is me. You have been asleep a long while."

The pitying tones of Peter's voice recalled the boy's trouble to his mind, and, flinging himself again on the ground, he sobbed as if his heart would break. "O Martin, Martin! why did you go away? Oh, I shall never be happy again now you are gone!"

The blacksmith waited till the burst of grief was over, feeling scarcely more equal to comfort the child's sorrow now, than he had done the first morning after Martin's departure. He had recourse to the same remedy now that he had used then—a strange one, seemingly, but after all the best for those in trouble: he sought, not in words of vain sympathy, but in active employment, in which self and sorrow is forgotten, to still the boy's passionate sorrow. "Come, Cock Robin," he said, when the sobs had somewhat subsided: "be a man, and don't be crying any more. I want you to do something for me, so get up and wash your face, and straighten yourself up a bit."

Robin had become so used to obey the kind but firm voice, that he almost instinctively did what he was told.

"Now," said Peter, when he had finished;
"go down and get some sticks and light up
the fire again; your mother has let it out,
poor woman, and she'll catch her death of
cold sitting there this bitter day, with a north
wind blowing fit to freeze you; and when
you've done that, if she doesn't want anything else, come down to the turnpike, where
I shall be waiting, for I want you to walk
across the common with me to Beverly Hol-
low before it gets dark."

Robin obeyed his orders, wondering a little
what had put it into Peter's head about the
fire, and, still more, what he could want at
Beverly so late in the day; and joined him
at last at the turnpike, looking considerably
brighter than when they parted.

"Now," said the blacksmith, as they
passed through the toll-gate; "sharp's the
word, my boy, or we shan't be home before
dark."

"What have you got to do at Beverly,
sir?"

"What should I have to do? have you
forgotten that to-day is Sunday?"

" Why are we going, then?"

" For the walk, to be sure! I suppose you don't see any use in a walk for nothing; but I do, a great deal. It'll do us both a world of good, see if it don't! besides which, a talk with you was just what I wanted."

" With *me*, sir?" said Robin, wonderingly.

"Yes, with you. You and I must be great friends now, Robin, as Martin's gone. Have you forgotten what he said the morning before he left us, about your taking his place to me? he and I used to take many a Sunday walk along this same road."

Robin was silent, a good deal puzzled at the blacksmith's manner. He talked so cheerfully of Martin, with a smile on his face as if nothing had happened, and he was still only away at a distance to return soon. And such was the case; for Peter thought of Martin as away in a land " very far off," whence, indeed, he should not return, but where they should, please God, one day join him. At last he said, doubtfully, " Please, sir, I don't think I could ever be like Martin."

" Why not?"

" I don't know; but he was a great friend of yours, wasn't he, sir?"

" Yes, that he was; and why shouldn't you be so, too? It seems to me we are very good friends already."

Robin did not reply, but there was a grateful look in his face that was sufficient answer.

They now walked on for some distance in silence, and then Peter said, " Your father's terribly cut up, poor man. He was very fond of Martin."

" O yes. I don't think he will ever be happy now he's gone. Oh, it was so dreadful when Wilson brought the news, he seemed half-mad like."

" It's a terrible trial; but, still, he's not so badly off as many. There is Mr. Fearon, our parson, up yonder: he lost his boy, as fine a young gent as ever was, and he had none to take his place. He was his only son."

" But I shall never be what Martin was to father."

"Why not? what was there in him that you can't be?"

"Oh, so many things. Father was so proud of him; and even mother, too, I think."

"And why should not they be proud of you too?"

"Proud of me!" Robin almost laughed at the idea. "Why, I ain't a bit like Martin."

"Not much, perhaps, now; but you may be some day if you try. Do you know, when you were asleep just now, I thought you looked very like him?"

"But he was so clever."

"That was chiefly because he stuck to his book at school, and tried to get on; and I don't see why you shouldn't, also."

"Well, I suppose I might," said Robin, thoughtfully; "but, oh! there were so many other things, so different from me. Somehow, things all seemed to go better when he was here. I heard father say once he'd be a deal better man if Martin was always by."

"Well," said Barnet, after a pause, "any-

how, you can be like him in some things, if
not in all: and then, perhaps, you'll find out
the other things in time. What do you say
to trying?"

"I don't think it would be any good."

"So you won't try? That's like a coward."

"Why a coward?" asked Robin, red-
dening.

"To be afraid to try what seems difficult.
How would it be if I said I couldn't shoe a
kicking horse?"

Robin laughed: "That wouldn't do, sir;
but how am I to begin?"

"What did we say, just now, about his
being clever, because he stuck to his book at
school? well, you might begin with that."

Robin made a wry face, and Peter
laughed. "I thought as much; book learning isn't much in your line? Well, that's a
pity, certainly; still, you might try, I think.
You might get to like it in time. Now let
us think what else you could do."

"I don't think there is anything else. I
don't remember much what Martin used to
do different from us, except go to church of

a Sunday. It wasn't so much what he *did*, as he himself, sir—I can't exactly say what I mean."

"All right: I understand. But there's this going to church of Sundays. Why can't you try that?"

"No," said Robin, with decision. "I don't want to go to church. I never went in my life, as I know of."

"Yes, you did, though, once, along with Martin and me, when you were ever so little. Didn't he ever take you again?"

"No; mother and neighbour Rixon, and Granny Scratchley, and ever so many others, used to laugh at him for going, and call him Parson Mat, but he didn't seem to mind; but I did, though, for one day I said I'd go with him, and they began at me, too, and said I was Parson Bob, and I couldn't stand it. I can't bear to be thought a fool, so I took and ran away, and never went again. I always kept out of the way on Sundays when it came near church time."

"What harm did it do you, their calling you that?"

"Well—well," said Robin, hesitating, and feeling rather at a loss for an answer; "I didn't like it."

"Well, I don't like taking nasty physic when I'm ill, nor doing hard work when I'm lazy; but it must be done, all the same. Was that all?"

"I don't think you'd like to be called such things," said Robin, a little hurt at his difficulties being made so light of. Peter burst out laughing.

"Why, I've been called Parson Sledge-hammer by half the village, ever since I can remember, and it's never done me any harm that I know of! Look here, Robin," he continued, more gravely: "what do you say to trying church to-night? the Beverly bells are ringing now, and then we can see what harm these dreadful names do you."

But Robin was by no means so easily convinced. "I don't like church," he said, resolutely.

"I thought you said you'd never been, so how can you know if you like it or not? Don't you want to be like Martin?"

" Yes, I'd like to be that."

" Well, you'll never be so if you don't go to church; and besides, if you are called nicknames for it, why, you'll be more like him than ever."

Robin laughed, and then they talked of other things till they reached Beverly church, where the bell had just done ringing ; and the blacksmith stopped at the lich-gate and said, smiling, " Well, old chap, shall it be Parson Bob and Parson Sledgehammer to-night, for the sake of Parson Mat ?"

And Robin nodded, with a smile on his lips and tears in his eyes, and they both went into church.

CHAPTER VI.

ROBIN'S PROSPECTS.

"He only knows, for He can read
  The mystery of the wicked heart,
Why vainly oft our arrows speed
  When aimed with most unerring art ;
While from some rude and powerless arm
  A random shaft, in season sent,
Shall light upon some lurking harm,
  And work some wonder little meant."

Two years passed away, bringing with them, as years ever will bring, joy and sorrow, hopes and fears, clouds and sunshine, to the people of Burnside. To Peter Barnet the years had brought few changes; still he worked on day by day, cheery and earnest, strong and gentle as ever. A few more hard lines on the brown face, a thread of silver here and there in the crisp black hair, a graver tone in the deep voice—these were all the traces of two years.

Robin Hill was now a tall, strong lad of

fifteen, much altered and improved in many ways. Many people said he was growing like Martin, but this was, perhaps, rather fanciful; or, if at all real, more so in his character than his outward appearance.

He still worked at the forge, and every day seemed a new link binding him and the blacksmith in a closer intimacy, silently, too, loosening his connection with his home; this, though so gradual as to be quite un-perceived by himself, became a daily source of disquiet to his friend. Robin's Sundays were now always passed away from home, and Peter could not tell how to discourage what he knew to be Robin's only chance of a quiet day and regular attendance at church. On week-days, too, the hours not spent at school were passed mostly at the forge; and when school-days were past, and Robin had to enter on life in earnest, Peter could not be surprised at the boy's earnest request to be allowed to enter for good into the service of his old master, whom he so dearly loved.

"I'll serve you honestly, master," said Robin, eagerly, as he made his request.

" Schoolmaster says I've been a good lad at
school, and he could get me a good place in
town, and father calls me a blockhead for
letting slip such a chance ; but I told them
both that, blockhead or not, I'd stick to you
if you'd have me ; for I don't believe there's
another in the world who'd have done all
you have for me."

" And what did your father say to that ?"
asked Peter, with a grave face.

" Say ! I don't know, sir, nor I don't
care, for I didn't stop to hear ; for he was
just in from the ' Feathers,' and I knew
what it would be, whatever I said to him.
He's always against you, master, for he
knows you are the best friend I have
got."

Peter's face grew graver still, as he heard
these words. " Ought this state of things
to continue ? Was not any little good he
might have done Robin counteracted by the
habit he was acquiring of disregarding his
father's wishes, of neglecting the home and
parents which God had given him, bad and
wretched as they might be ? Peter was

E 2

sadly puzzled. On the one hand his affection and care for his young charge inclined him to bid him remain under his own eye, doing the work for which he was evidently best suited, and leading such a life of simple, honest labour as his own had been. On the other hand was what, perhaps, might be a good opening in the town, in a large warehouse, where he would be almost alone among strangers—hasty of temper, weak of purpose, easily led into temptation; the prospect was at best a doubtful one to the prudent blacksmith. Then, too, he knew well that Hill's opposition to Robin's will arose, not from any real care for his welfare, but from jealous dislike to himself, and pleasure in anything that he thought might annoy him.

"I wish I could see a bit clearer," thought Peter. "It seems hard, when the lad has taken to one so, and seems so to wish like to settle down steady and honest in the place where he was born and bred, that he should not have his way; and I never did hold with the young fellows rushing off to the town

there : there's many a one I've know'd rue
the day as he left his native place. For my
part, it seems to me that the old smithy's a
safe place, if there is one in this world ; but
there, that ain't saying much." At length,
after many debatings with himself, Peter
told Robin that he would think the matter
over, and set off to the rectory to consult
Mr. Fearon, whom he felt sure would know
best what he ought to do.

The clergyman listened with much interest to Peter as he related the history of his
connection with Robin Hill, and laid his
present difficulty before him ; and then, with
a few simple words, set the blacksmith's mind
at rest as to the right course to pursue.

" I can quite understand," he said, " your
natural wish to keep this poor boy with you ;
and indeed, as far as I can see, he seems far
more fitted for such a life than one of greater
trial. But we must never forget our first
duty to Him who said, ' Children, obey your
parents in all things, for this is right.' It
cannot be your duty to teach Robin disobe-
dience to this plain command."

"In *all* things!" repeated Peter, doubt-fully.

"In all things—that is, where we can do so without sinning against our Heavenly Father, who is, of course, first of all. But you must remember, Barnet, that going into Mr. Benson's service is no sin; many would even think it almost a duty to accept such a good offer. The establishment is, I believe, respectable, and the pay better than you could give him."

"It may be wrong to say so, sir," cried Peter, impatiently, "but it ain't the lad's welfare that Hill is thinking of; if it were, I'd be the last to say a word against it."

"Stay, my friend," said the rector, kindly; "what his motives may be does not concern us. Ought we not rather to be thankful for any opportunity of teaching the boy obedience to his father, even though it may not be quite in the way we should have chosen?"

"It isn't as if he cared for the lad," mur-mured Peter, still but half convinced.

"Well, if he does not, perhaps it may be

settled as you wish. But I think, if you consider a little, you will see that there is reason in what I have said. The self-denial will be good for Robin. It may be the means of teaching father and son their mutual duties, and you must forgive me, Barnet, if I say that it may also be good for you."

"You're right there, sir," said Peter, humbly. "I believe I've been thinking of myself pretty near as much as Robin; for I can't a-bear to part with him, sir, especially thinking of him, so young and lonesome like, among all them strangers."

"Not alone, Barnet, while he has the Best Friend of all; and we can always pray for him. Now, however, I must bid you good-night, as I see it is getting late. You must think it over, and I have little doubt you will see it as I do."

"I believe I do already, sir; though it don't come quite easy yet. Good-night, sir, and thank you, kindly." And Peter walked off, with a mind considerably relieved.

His way back was past Hill's cottage; and as he neared it the sound of voices, in angry dispute, which he soon recognised as those of Robin and his father, made him stop to listen. Hill had evidently been drinking, and his voice sounded hoarse with passion. "You won't obey me, won't you, you young rascal? You shall, though, as sure as my name is Hill. I'll go up to that beggarly old blacksmith, and give him a piece of my mind—see if I don't!"

"Well, go if you like," came Robin's answer, his voice shaking with anger; "but it'll be on a fool's errand; for I won't be driven to it by any one—not as Master Barnet could listen to such as you. He'll take me whenever I ask him, spite of all you say."

"Aye, parson was right," thought Barnet, sadly, as he turned away, too grieved to hear more. "It seems like a judgment on me; and yet, God knows I meant to do my duty. But there, we're poor blind folks, all of us! Maybe we'll find out the right way some day!"

CHAPTER VII.

THE BLACKSMITH'S VISITOR.

" Judge not the Lord by feeble sense,
    But trust Him for His grace
    Behind a frowning providence
    He hides a smiling face.

" His purposes will ripen fast,
    Unfolding every hour;
    The bud may have a bitter taste,
    But sweet will be the flower."

Six o'clock the following evening found
Robin Hill entering his father's cottage.
There was something in the boy's face—a
look sad, yet of unwonted gentleness—that
made his parents (who, for a wonder, were
both at home) turn from their disputes to
look at him.

" Well, what's the matter now?" asked
Mrs. Hill, sharply; and then, being interrupted by a volley of abuse from her husband, showered on the unlucky boy, she left

the cottage, too little interested to remain, and glad to leave them to fight it out alone.

" Been mooning about after that old vagabond Barnet again, I suppose. But it shan't be much longer, I can tell you."

" No, I don't suppose it *will* be much longer," said Robin, with a sigh.

" What do you mean by that? Some fresh impudence, I'll be bound."

" I mean, father," said Robin, quietly, " that I don't suppose I shall see much more of Master Barnet, or of any one else here either, if I am to go to Benson's; for I suppose I shall have to go at once, or it will be filled up."

" You *will* go, then, after all?" said Hill, eyeing his son with bewilderment.

" Yes, father, I will go."

" What's this change for, all of a sudden? What makes you say you will go?"

" Because you wish it."

" *I?*—I didn't know you cared for what *I* thought."

Robin did not reply; he only stood bending

over the table, trying to hide the tears that would come springing to his eyes, as he strove hard to remember the blacksmith's counsel he had just received, and to listen patiently to his father. Hill, too, remained silent : turning over, for the first time, the thought suggested by Robin's last reply, " Because *you* wish it." Now, for the first time, he realised (though even yet but dimly) that, as his father, Robin's future depended mainly upon himself; with the first acknowledgment of the son's duty came the first thought of the father's. The new idea puzzled him, and he hardly knew whether to be angry or pleased with it.

" You 've been having a row with that blacksmith fellow," he said at last, sullenly enough.

Robin's eye sparkled with ill-suppressed anger, but he managed to answer, calmly, " No, father ; Master Barnet's the best friend I ever had, and it's he as told me to bide by what you say."

" *He* told you ! " exclaimed Hill, now thoroughly astonished and puzzled. " What's that for, now, I wonder? He was never a friend of mine, as I know of."

" Well," said Robin,—his small stock of patience fast ebbing away under his father's surly reception of what was to him a real piece of self-denial,—" all I know is, that I wished to go to the forge, and I believe he wished it too, but he said as he'd never take me on against your will; and I suppose he's right." And with these words Robin left the room.

What did it all mean? Robert Hill puzzled over it sadly, as he sat alone in his cottage. He, the drunken good-for-nothing spend-thrift, whom every respectable person in the place regarded with contempt, to be raised suddenly to the position of decider in what, now he came to think of it, was no light matter. To have his wishes consulted, his opinion given way to, not only by his formerly rebellious son but by Peter Barnet, who he had regarded almost as an enemy. He could make nothing out of it, and yet he could not help feeling it right, and as it should be, for Robin to come to his father, as the first to be consulted. As he looked back on his own childhood, he could remember his careful father watching over his boy's welfare, working hard to keep his family in comfort and respectability, sending his sons to school, and never resting till they were out in the world, earning their living honestly. Then came, with a strange pang, the thought of what followed that good father's death; and Hill started up and left the cottage hastily.

For some time he walked on hurriedly, taking almost instinctively the road to the "Feathers," where he was wont to drown his bitter thoughts in drink. At last he came to where a side road led up the hill to the old forge, and here (perhaps almost for the first time) Hill paused, not certain which way to turn. Robin's conduct had puzzled and excited him, rousing him for a time from his usual state of apathetic indifference. " I can't make it out," he said to himself, half angrily. " I've half a mind to go myself and have it out with that old bear up yonder. I don't half like all this chopping and changing. There's something underhand as I don't fancy." And muttering these words, half defiant, half sullen, Robert Hill, for the first time, chose the forge before the " Feathers." Strangely, indeed, come these turning-points in our lives. It is often said that our first steps on the downward path are taken with our eyes closed. Almost as often, I think, is the first step on the heavenward road taken in the same way, in blindness and ignorance, feeling not in the dark the strong Hand guiding us to our home; and it is only of God's pity that when we *do* see the way we do not turn back again to our ruin.

Work had been over for some time, but still Peter Barnet sat in the forge over his dying fire, sunk in deep, anxious thought over what had happened that day. His interview with Robin that afternoon had not been satisfactory. The boy had for some time refused to listen to him, accusing him of unkindness and injustice, and at last he left him, with only a reluctant half-promise not to oppose his father, and Peter knew Robin's hasty temper well enough to fear an outbreak on the first provocation; and now the blacksmith sat in the fading light, alternately torn by fear for Robin and self-reproach for not speaking with more effect, when his thoughts were interrupted by a step at the door, and a rough voice calling his name.

" Hill, *you* here !" Peter exclaimed, astonished, as he recognised his unusual visitor.

"Aye—you didn't much expect me here, nor wish for me, either," was the sulky answer.

Peter was perplexed what to make of it all, but his natural kindness prompted him to say, cheerfully, " Well, come in, man— don't stand out there ! If there's anything I can do for you I will ; only come in, and say what it is."

" *You* do for me ! Much you'd be willing to do for me, I should think," said Hill, with a sneer. " No, I ain't come to that yet ; I only want a word with you about that rascal boy of mine."

"Robin ? If it's anything to do with him, come in, I say, so much the more. That young chap is a friend of mine, as I dare say you know, and what concerns him concerns us both; so come in, and we'll talk it over. Wait a bit, though, till we've got a bit of fire;" and so saying, Barnet set to work on the bellows, till in a few minutes the forge was once more full of ruddy light.

Hill stood watching him in silence, not quite knowing how to begin; for somehow each puff of the bellows, each warmer, brighter glow, seemed to drive out of his mind all the cutting things he had meant to say of Robin and his friend. Presently Peter paused in his work, and, scrutinising the heavy sullen face made visible by the warm blaze, began,—

"I'm right glad to see you here, Master Hill!"

"Not much cause for that," was the sulky reply.

"I don't know about that. I thought you came to talk of the boy."

"So I do. I don't half like his goings on. I don't understand them; and what's more," he continued, more vigorously now the ice was broken, "I won't have it, for all you may say, Master Barnet."

"Why, what's the lad been up to now?"

"Now!" echoed Hill; "What's he been up to this year past? that's what I want to know?"

"Why, growing as fine a young fellow as ever walked, to be sure. Why, he's his dead brother come to life again, I tell you."

The allusion to Martin opened a subject in which both men were interested, and, almost in spite of himself, Hill found himself comparing notes with the blacksmith on the son who, through all his own backslidings, he had still been proud of; on his cleverness, his handsome person and winning manner, his favour with the gentry, his good prospects; even at last, with natural emotion, on his sad and sudden death.

Thus nearly an hour passed almost unnoticed by the two men, spent in friendly chat on a subject on which both liked to dwell, which otherwise would have been wasted by Hill with vicious comrades at the "Feathers," till at last the striking of the clock reminded them of the flight of time.

"Why, here we've been a whole hour,"

F

exclaimed Peter, laughing; "and now I don't know what you came for, Master Hill."

"Well, I'd pretty nigh forgot it myself. But as we are on it now, I want to know what you've been saying to that boy, for he's one too many for me, with his saying this and that. Why, there he is one minute storming and blustering, because I say he's to go to Benson's, right out of this wretched hole, where every one thinks themselves above the likes of us; and now here he is saying just the contrary, and sticking to it as you won't take him on, the young liar!"

"Stop" said Peter, gravely; "don't miscall the lad without cause. What he said was true. I won't take him on, or any other boy who comes against his parents' wishes. Not as I think him wrong in wishing to bide here. I tell you frankly, Hill, I would not send a boy of mine in a hurry to Benson's, or anywhere in the town, without I knew some one would keep an eye on him. Robin's a good lad, but he's a boy after all; and then, too, he's got a will for the old trade here,

and would make a good smith in time. But
that's neither here nor there. His father's
the first and nearest to him, and you know
best, or *ought* to know what's best for your
own flesh and blood."

Hill looked up quickly as his ear caught
the emphasis which Barnet almost unconsciously laid on the word " ought;" and the
old sullen expression came into his face as he
answered, impatiently, "There, have done
with your preaching, do, for I won't stand it.
I don't know what right you have to meddle
with my affairs, or the boy's either. I
suppose if I don't choose to have him always
dangling about after you, I'm not obliged
to, am I?"

"No," said Barnet, quietly; "I don't
suppose you are. But don't lose your
temper over it. The boy is yours to do
what you like with. If you think best to
send him to Benson's, well and good. It's
good pay and good quarters, I'm told, and
there's many a one would think himself
lucky to get such a chance."

"Ah! that's just it," said Hill, recovering

his temper under the soothing sense of having done something sharp in his choice for Robin; "there's just the point. I'm a bit sharper than you thought me, and can see a good thing when it comes. Perhaps, when Bob comes back with his pockets full of money, you won't think Robert Hill such a fool after all."

Barnet could hardly repress a smile at the foolish boast; but, vain and empty as it was, a thought of gratitude still rose in his heart, as he, for the first time, saw the father interested in his son's welfare, and drawing bright pictures for the future.

"Ah well!" he replied, cheerfully, "I hope it'll be as you say. And now, as you've settled it to your liking, I hope you won't think me meddlesome if I say, that if any ways I could be of any use to you, or the boy, I'd be glad to be so. I don't know much of Benson's myself; and if you don't either, I think it would be as well to find out a little about it, before sending Robin there in too much hurry."

"Right enough," said Hill, feeling ashamed

of his churlishness, as he heard Barnet's kind words. " But," he continued, doubt-fully, " I don't rightly know how to set about it. That schoolmaster as told him of it ain't no friend of mine, and——"

" There, don't trouble about that. If you'll just leave it to me, I'll step down there myself to-morrow evening—leastways if you think well of my doing so—and ask him all particulars, and then let you know, and you could see what you think of it."

" I'm sure you're very kind."

" No, I ain't: it's no trouble. Perhaps you'd step in here again to-morrow night, or"—as he saw Hill hesitate for an answer—" I'll look into your place myself, on the chance of finding you in, and if things seem favourable I'll take my pipe with you, and we'll talk it over."

Hill raised no objection to this very un-expected proposal, though he did not very cordially assent to it; and soon after took his leave, and walked home with his head full of many strange new feelings. His talk with Barnet had pleased and flattered him:

he felt of more importance than before : the
notion of performing a duty, which to most
fathers comes naturally, was to him a fresh
and on the whole a rather pleasant sensation.
His vanity was gratified by being given way
to by a man like Barnet, who in his secret
heart he respected, and even feared ;- and
the blacksmith's admiration for Martin, and
affection for Robin, made him feel that his
sons were children to be proud of.   With
these feelings, too, were largely mingled un-
easiness and self-reproach.   He felt that he
really had no good or sufficient reason for
wishing to send Robin to Benson's.   His re-
solution had been first taken out of spite, and
strengthened by the opposition he had met
with.   But now (as generally happens) when
he had gained his point, he began to see the
folly of it.   He knew that Robin was sorely
disappointed, and that Barnet's sense and
judgment pointed strongly to keeping the
boy in a position where he could not fall into
the way of any grievous temptation or mischief.   But still his pride and obstinacy could
not thus be at once overcome by his clearer

reason; and his last words to Robin that night, before retiring (sober, for a wonder) to rest, were, " You 'd best make up your mind to Benson's; for you are going there, whether you like it or not ! "

CHAPTER VIII.

ANOTHER VISIT.

"The herbs we seek to heal our woe,
  Familiar round our pathway grow:
  Our common air is balm."

IT was with unfeigned pleasure and astonish-
ment that Robin heard from his father of
the blacksmith's intended visit the following
evening.   He would much have liked to ask
the cause of this unwonted event; but he
refrained from questions, fearing to offend
his father, and so disturb the unusual quiet-
ness which had existed in the household all
day. This tranquillity had been brought
about by several causes. Mrs. Hill had been
for some time suffering from a neglected
cold, which, during the last few days, had increased so rapidly that she was now quite
unable to leave her bed, but lay able to do
little more than turn her head from side to
side, moaning, or feebly complaining of the

pain she suffered. Robin had attended to her as best he could, watching patiently beside her, and doing all in his power to relieve her. Seeing that she grew no better, and alarmed at her laboured breathing and evident suffering, he had urged her to send for the doctor; but this she refused to do, fretfully declaring she wanted no meddling doctors, nor medicine to poison her, either. At last, however, in the afternoon, Robin determined to take the matter into his own hands, and went to Mr. Crofton, who, much to his disappointment, he found out, and not likely to return till late that night. The man, however, promised that he would tell his master directly he returned; and that if he could not come to Mrs. Hill that night, he should do so the first thing next day. In the evening, however, she seemed easier, and Robin began to hope that his fears were unfounded, and to look forward with unclouded pleasure to Peter Barnet's visit. What with his mother's illness, and his father's unusual silence and abstraction when he returned from work, the cottage was, for that day at least, in an unusually peaceful condition; and as the hour for Peter's coming approached, Robin, leaving his mother asleep, busied himself with trying to make the shabby cottage present a more cheerful appearance. This was by no means an easy matter. The fire must be relighted and coaxed into a blaze, the furniture arranged as tidily as its dilapidated state would allow, his father's tools and cast-off working clothes put away, and dust, cobwebs, and rubbish removed from the corners. Robin wondered, as one thing after another presented itself to his anxious eyes, how it was that the wretchedness of his home had never struck him before; and the same thought even suggested itself to his father, who stood silently watching him (not, as usual, grumbling at what he considered fuss), but wandering restlessly in and out, casting uneasy glances up the road.

At length Robin's labours were complete, though by no means to his own satisfaction, and the father and son stood together on the hearth.

"I hope he'll be here soon," said Robin, looking doubtfully at his father.

"I ain't a-going to stay in all night for him," was the morose answer; "I half wish I'd not asked him."

Robin knew better than to suggest a different opinion, and presently his father continued: "It's more than I can make out now, and I suppose I'm being taken in some way. But I'll show him I'm not such a fool as he thinks. I know he thinks he'll come round me with his buttering ways, and have you poking all your life in this wretched place, as has been my ruin and will be yours too."

He had no time to say more, for at this moment Peter's knock was heard at the door, and Robin sprang forward to welcome him.

Hill received his guest awkwardly enough, but a few of Peter's cordial words seemed to set everything right; and in a short time the two men were sitting over their pipes, chatting as cosily as possible. Robin joined little in the talk, even though it so nearly concerned himself. It was quite enough for him to sit watching the blacksmith's kindly, genial face, and to assure himself again and again that it was no dream, but a delightful reality.

Peter's report of his interview with the schoolmaster was, on the whole, satisfactory; and at first sight Mr. Benson's place seemed all that could be desired. The situation was as under-porter in the large upholstery establishment of Benson & Co. The pay was good, the work not heavy, though regular; there was prospect of speedy advancement to a higher post; and Mr. Benson's well-known reputation as a large, highly respectable, and most prosperous firm, was of great advantage to a youth first starting in life. There were many applicants for the place, but Mr. Sharp, being well acquainted with the head of the firm, knew well that a strong recommendation from himself would go far to secure it to Robin.

So far all was fair enough; but there are some persons who look beyond mere worldly

prosperity, and Peter was one of these. He
knew that Mr. Benson's one thought was
gain—that his whole heart was wrapped up
in his business. He could remember the
time when young Benson set up on his own
account, toiling night and day to out-do and
beat his rivals in trade out of the field;
sticking at no underhand dealing, no meanly-
taken advantage, that could advance his own
selfish interests. And now that his end was
gained, and he was a rich and thriving man,
the same idea pervaded his dealings. His
servants were chosen because they were
good men of business, sharp at a bargain,
quick at seeing their own advantage. A
respectable exterior and general character
for honesty were indeed necessary for the
respectability of the firm, but beyond this no
questions were asked. The servant's per-
sonal character out of working hours was
nothing to his employer. If Robin went
there his evenings and Sundays were entirely at his own disposal, most likely spent
with his companions in the warehouse, many
of whom Peter well knew to be men calcu-

lated to do grievous mischief to Robin's easy and pliable disposition.

However, these latter considerations were quite out-weighed, in Robert Hill's eyes, by the brilliancy of the former; indeed, had the place appeared less promising, he had so set his heart on gaining his point, that he would have been little, if at all, influenced by matters concerning the service of that higher Master, whom for years he had forgotten.

Peter told him frankly his own opinion of the affair; but finding it weighed nothing, but only rather irritated Hill, he said no more on the subject, trusting that Robin's ultimate good would be brought about in some way he did not yet understand. "I can't see it all yet" he said to himself, reverting to his old comfort when in difficulty; "but we're blind folk, groping in the dark, and the Almighty knows what's good for the lad better than I do."

Some good was, however, already apparent even in the seeming evil. To have aroused Hill from his selfish indifference was a step

gained, and more than this was accomplished
as the preparations for Robin's departure
went on towards completion. A better un-
derstanding already existed between father
and son, though Robin still felt his disappointment, and Hill felt secretly ashamed of
his obstinacy. Robin was learning, unconsciously, to turn more for advice to his
natural adviser, and Hill found himself often
obliged, out of very shame at his own ignorance, to take counsel of the blacksmith.

There was much to be done and thought
of : Mr. Sharp had to be asked for a recommendation ; then Mr. Benson had to be
personally applied to, and this was no easy
matter, as there were many other candidates
for the place, and Mr. Benson's time was
too fully occupied to allow much of it for
seeing the various comers. Many an hour
was spent by father and son waiting patiently
in the little counting-house, and, as is
often the case, the difficulty of obtaining the
place made it appear more desirable to both ;
even Robin at length becoming anxious for
it, if only to please his father, whom he saw

was becoming daily more bent on it. Peter Barnet, too, could not fail to rejoice over the evenings stolen, as it were, from the "Feathers" and devoted to an object which, if not the best, was at least in some respects a good one.

At last, however, the destined end was gained, and Robin (not without some satisfaction) brought Peter the news that he had gained the place, and was to be in his new post the Monday fortnight following.

"And what does your father say?" asked Peter.

"I never knew him so pleased about anything, master. He's gone up to tell Mr. Sharp about it himself. Do you know, I'm glad of it myself now?"

"That's a good job, anyhow."

"Well, I think so too. But yet it's not because I want a bit the less to bide with you, but seeing father pleased is worth something."

"So it is, my lad; and, please God, he may have still better cause to be pleased, if you keep steady and do your duty."

That fortnight was an important one to the Hills, for it left Robin motherless. Her own carelessness, and poor Robin's inexperienced nursing, soon made Mrs. Hill's illness take a most serious form, and at last the doctor pronounced her case hopeless. The news came like a thunderclap on her husband, who had been too much absorbed in Robin's affairs to pay much heed to her danger. Then, as he stood with his sobbing son beside the bed of death, came with a shock the too late remorse for his share in the discomforts of their married life. He thought of his first wife, Martin's gentle mother, and with what different feelings he had closed her eyes, turned on him so lovingly even in death, and how he had heard her last faint prayer for him and their little son. Ah! how ill had her wishes been fulfilled!

Mr. Fearon had, at Robin's earnest request, visited Mrs. Hill constantly during her illness, and his prayers and counsels had done much to soften and bring her to repentance.

Now, as she lay free from pain but sinking

fast, she spoke with deep humility of her many sins. "I've been a bad wife and a bad mother," she said; " but I ask your pardon, and your father's too ; and Mr. Fearon says God is merciful." She could say no more than this, as weakness prevented her from speaking, but her last moments were quiet, though sad, and she died with her hand in her husband's and her eyes fixed on her son, who stood crying bitterly beside her.

Thus, for the second time, death visited the Hills; and, as on the former occasion, the blacksmith came to the hushed house, hoping to be of some help to the mourners—not, however, as before, to be rejected in sullen despair, but received as a welcome friend. Not that any of the party talked much. Robin was overcome by passionate, boyish grief; Hill was subdued and silent, and Peter would not interfere with their natural grief. The evening passed quietly, both father and son feeling soothed and cheered by Peter's genial presence and few and quiet but sincere words of sympathy.

The funeral took place on the following Friday, two days before Robin's departure. No one followed the coffin to the grave except her husband and son, and the blacksmith; for Mrs. Hill had made few friends during her life, and of these so-called friends few cared for her sufficiently to pay this last tribute of respect where no respect had been felt. Many of the more respectable of the place wondered, as they said, to see Master Barnet lowering himself to be mixed up with such a bad lot as the Hills; but Peter cared for nothing that was said : his only feelings were of awe and humility in the near presence of death, and anxiety to lighten in any way the sorrow of those more nearly concerned.

"It's a sad farewell to your home, my lad, I know," said Barnet, kindly, as he parted from Robin and his father after the service was over. " But I'm sure all as we've been hearing this afternoon 'll bide long in our thoughts and be a comfort to us."

With these words Peter left them, and then father and son went home together, bound closer to each other than ever before by the new tie of a common sorrow.

Remembering Peter's old maxim, that work is sorrow's best cure, Robin soon busied himself, on reaching home, in preparing tea and putting the cottage in order, at which during his mother's illness he had become quite an adept; trying by cheerful talk to turn his father's thoughts from the sad sense of silence and emptiness which death always leaves in a house, however little the lost one's presence may have been valued during life.

"Now, father," he said at length, cheerily, drawing an arm-chair close to the brightly-blazing fire; "come and tell me if this isn't a first-rate strong cup of tea,"

"You're a good lad, Bob," said Hill, as he sat down, "and almost a woman for looking after the tea. I don't know where you get it from, I'm sure, unless it's from Barnet, where you get most good things from, seemingly. Not from your mother! she didn't know what a good cup of tea meant, poor soul. No—it's more like the old days, when

Martin was a little chap, and his mother used to make the place so tidy like, against I was home from work."

"Ah! I should like to hear about them," said Robin; "here, I'll reach down your pipe, and we'll try and be comfortable. But you must drink my tea first, or it'll be cold; you know I shan't make many more cups for you, before I go."

The words seemed like an echo to Hill's own sad thoughts, and he burst out suddenly —"Ah, Bob, my lad! I wish to goodness you weren't going. You're the last I have, and I can't a-bear to part with you just now, when I'm so lonesome, like. I'm half-way gone to ruin as it is, and I shall go the other half when I'm alone. I wish to goodness I'd never sent you after the place. It was only to spite Barnet—obstinate fool that I was! and now I've only punished myself."

Robin tried to comfort his father as best he could, assuring him that all was for the best, and that the blacksmith would still remain to be a friend to him; but even as he spoke a pang seemed to come at his heart as he thought: "Oh! would he only have spoken the truth sooner." What would he not have given to be able to go to Peter and tell him he was free to follow his wishes? But it seemed too late: the engagement was made, and he could not, he thought, draw back.

"Never mind, father dear," he said, gently; "it can't be helped now. I'm sure it's true what Master Barnet says, that all is for the best, though we can't see it all clear at once."

CHAPTER IX.

GOOD NEWS.

" He maketh the storm to cease,
So that the waves thereof are still."

ALL is, indeed, for the best! And so, a few
hours later, would Robin and his father say,
with feelings of joyful gratitude to Him who
does all things well.

Hardly had the words with which I con-
clude my last chapter passed Robin's lips,
when, without his ordinary knock for admis-
sion, Peter Barnet entered the cottage, a
letter in his hand, his face full of a wonderful
happiness.

" Master Barnet! You here! What is
it? Is anything the matter?" were the
questions poured forth simultaneously by
both father and son; but they could get no
answer, for the worthy blacksmith only threw
himself into a chair, and, tossing the letter to
Robin, absolutely burst into tears, exclaim-

ing, "There, it's too much! I can't help
it! Oh, thank God for His goodness to
us!"

Robin took the letter, and examined its
strange stamp and post-marks in perplexity,
till at last, with a cry of joy, he almost
screamed, " Martin !"

Yes, it was indeed Martin—the lost found,
the dead alive again ; Martin himself, speaking in every line of that long, eagerly-read
letter.

For a long time neither of the three could
do more than try to realise the happy truth.
Robin, crying and laughing together ; Hill,
staring at the envelope, and rubbing his
eyes to assure himself that it was no dream ;
Barnet, repeating again and again, " It's
true; he's alive! Our Martin's alive and
well!"

At last, however, composure sufficient
was recovered for the blacksmith to read the
letter, which was addressed to himself, as
the one Martin felt most sure of receiving
it gladly.   It contained full particulars of the
shipwreck, and told how, though thought by

every one to be lost, he had escaped with
one or two brave comrades on a raft roughly
constructed from the timbers of the sinking
ship ; how, after terrible sufferings, they had
been picked up half-dead by a foreign vessel
bound for South America, where they had
been obliged to remain some time before
they could get a ship to carry them to their
right destination. Here fresh trials awaited
him. His place was filled up, and he had
much difficulty in obtaining employment.
He had delayed writing home, hoping to
give a better account of himself in a short
time ; and when he at last did so, the ship
carrying his letter had been partially de-
stroyed by fire, and the news had never
reached England. Some months again
elapsed before he heard of this disaster, and
then various other causes again prevented
his writing. Now, however, the good news
contained in his letter made up for all past
silence. He had obtained an excellent ap-
pointment near Melbourne, and was already
in the way of becoming a very prosperous
man. "And now, my dear friend," he said,

in conclusion, "after all that has happened
to me, you may guess how anxious I feel to
hear of you all at home. Every day I long
to hear of your safety and well-being; even
during those terrible days when I thought all
hope gone, I often asked God that we might
meet in heaven; and now that a new hope
is given me, that we may perhaps meet
again in this world, I long all the more for
news of you. As to Robin, I feel sure that
if (as I always hoped) you have been the
same friend to him as to me, he at least is
doing well. Tell him, with my best love,
that Cock Robin is seldom out of my
thoughts—never out of my prayers. Tell
him I shall always think of him, working
with you at the old trade (I always like to
think of him as a blacksmith), growing up,
perhaps, a second Master Barnet, making
the name of Hill honoured and respected by
all in our village. I sometimes wish to see
him; but I think England is safer for him,
and especially under your good care. And
as to my dear father—O Peter, I can speak
freely to you of the sadness that seems to

oppress me as I think of him. My only
hope is, that his eyes may have been opened
to see the better way, and to follow it. I
scarcely know what message to send him,
except my love both to him and my step-
mother. If, however, you should think it
well to do so, tell him, that for many weeks
the wish to have him near me has been
gaining strength in my heart. I fear, after
all the past, that Burnside is but a sad place
for him, and even now he may be feeling
that his good name is gone there, and cannot
be retrieved; but here, among strangers,
a new beginning might be made. Work is
plentiful, pay is good, and my position here
would ensure him a life of comfort and respectability. My mother, too, might obtain
employment easily, but I think she would
find housekeeping for us enough to do, and
looking after my bit of garden, and the cow
and poultry. I fear this is only a pleasant
dream of mine, too good for accomplish-
ment; but there can be no harm in men-
tioning it to you, my dear old friend. I leave
it to you to speak of it to my father. Now,

good-bye, and may God's blessing be with
you and all my dear friends at home.

"I am ever your faithful friend,

"MARTIN HILL."

No one spoke for some time after Peter
had finished reading this letter, and little
more was said that evening on the subject,
but all three thought deeply over what they
had heard. To Hill, especially, it formed
subject for very serious thought. Martin's
words had, for the first time, brought him
face to face with the fact of how entirely his
misconduct had taken away his good name
in the village. As he thought over it, he
could not but see how few of the respectable
Burnside people ever associated with him;
how the friends of his younger and better
days had one by one dropped away from
him, and had been replaced by others of low
and vicious character.

As he sat late that night in his cottage,
thinking over it all in silence and solitude,
his head sank lower and lower on his breast,
and a groan of anguish broke from his lips.

The same thought haunted his sleep, and mingled with his dreams that night; wherever he turned, he seemed to see the faces of his neighbours, full of contempt and dislike, and the sad eyes of his first wife looking at him with sorrowful reproach. But as the morning broke, he fell into a peaceful slumber, dreaming only of Martin smiling on him with his calm eyes, and beckoning him to come. He rose in the morning with a new hope (suggested by his son's letter) of a new beginning, a new country, a new life; and his first step was to consult the blacksmith. Peter entered readily into the subject, but advised that nothing should be done in haste, and at last induced Hill to go with him to Mr. Fearon, whom he thought would be the best person to consult, and the most likely to see the matter in its right light.

The rector's face was grave when he heard the unexpected announcement that Robert Hill wished to see him, but it soon brightened as he saw who was with him. He sympathised cordially when he heard the joyful news of Martin's restoration. " I suppose it is this happy news which has brought you here," he said, turning to Hill; " and I am very glad it has done so, and hope it will be by no means your last visit. You will be always most welcome to any help I can give you; I only wish you had oftener come before."

Hill was silent, not well knowing how to answer this undeserved kindness.

" It wasn't only on that account, sir," said Barnet, at last ; " Master Hill, here, is in a bit of a fix, and I told him as how I thought you'd help him."

" To be sure I will, if I can, if he will let me know what it it is."

There was a short pause, and then Hill began, awkwardly enough, stopping often for a word : " You see, sir, my boy here's alive and well, and you're welcome to read it all, though it ain't me as he wrote to; and somewhere on the last sheet you'll see as he wants me to go out there, for to make a new beginning like. I don't rightly remember his words, but you'll see them for yourself. It were a new beginning, I know," said poor Hill, repeating the words that had taken such hold of him, and then stopped, not knowing how to go on. Mr. Fearon's expression of kindly interest had altered to one of most earnest compassion and sympathy during Hill's speech, and his voice was full of kindness as he spoke. "A new beginning—ah, Hill, you are right to think of that, above all the rest; and God be thanked for giving you, after so many years, the chance of a new beginning. May He give you grace to make it with a new heart and new strength, to serve and please Him in newness of life, to the glory of His holy name."

These solemn words were followed by silence, during which Mr. Fearon read Martin's letter, the substance of which, however, he already knew. At length Barnet asked, "Then you think well of it, sir?"

"Indeed I do; but nothing should be done hastily. If, however, you will think it over again, and still find your opinion unaltered, I will do my best to set you in the right way of accomplishing your plan. One

thing, however, I think you have forgotten,
and that is, Robin.   Martin seems under a
false impression as to what his future life is
to be.   I trust, Hill, you have thought well
over this, for it is a grave responsibility.   Are
you sure you are leaving your boy in safe
hands?"

Hill was silent for a moment, and then
said, with an effort, " I know, sir, as I've no
right to ask the favour of you; I know I'm
his father, and ought to know best, but I fear
I'm not much to go by in these things, and
the young chap would have a poor chance
if he had only me to go by for what's best.
You see, sir, I've gone so wrong on my
own account like, I don't like to be trusting
myself on his.   So, sir, if you'd be so good,
I'd be thankful if you'd tell me what is best
to do."

A few inquiries as to Robin's wishes and
capabilities soon decided Mr. Fearon's answer
to this request.   " I think," he said, smiling,
"we had better go to Martin again for counsel.
I think he is as right in advising Robin to
stick to the old place and old trade as in

wishing you to leave all behind and begin afresh. You would wish, I think, to leave your son under a kind master, and among friends. Well, I don't think you could choose a better master or friend than Peter here; and," he added, smiling, " I think Robin will always find at least one other friend at the parsonage."

It is scarcely necessary to add, that Robin Hill's engagement with Benson was cancelled, and a fresh one entered on with his old master.

CHAPTER X.

GOOD-BYE.

" Christians !   We here may meet no more.
But there is yet a happier shore ;
And there, released from toil and pain,
Dear brethren, may we meet again."

MY story is drawing to a close; but there
are still some few words to be said of Robin
and his friends before concluding.

The arrangements for Hill's departure took
some time to make, and it was some months
before he actually left England.

Martin had to be informed of his father's
decision, and his letter of joyful welcome to
be awaited.   Then an emigrant ship had to
be found, and the money raised to pay his
passage out.   The old cottage and furniture
were sold for this purpose, and Mr. Fearon
and many others gladly contributed to so
good an object.

Robin's delight at the change in his prospects may be better imagined than described; but even this was (like all earthly pleasures) clouded by a new sorrow in the loss of his father.

Since Mrs. Hill's death the affection between father and son had increased and strengthened daily. The mother's death had been a common sorrow; Martin's restoration, a common joy; Peter Barnet, a common object of friendship and affection. Home, too, had become a word dear to both; and Barnet would often laughingly declare that it drew away the son from the forge, as much as it did the father from the " Feathers."

But, at last, the parting came, and a very sad one it was. Robin and Peter both accompanied Hill to Portsmouth, where they were to take leave of him; and poor Robin felt very sad and lonely as he saw the great ship move slowly out of the harbour, which was bearing his father away from him.

For a long time he stood motionless, watching first his father's figure on the deck, then the vessel growing smaller and smaller, till it was only a speck on the vast ocean. At last it was gone, and he could see only a track of golden light stretching across the shining sea almost from his feet to where the crimson sunset clouds touched the blue waves.

In after years, when Robin thought of his father, the scene came back to him, and the track of light seemed like bright memory, and the heaven to which it led like still brighter hope.

At last he was aroused from his musing by the blacksmith's voice at his side: "Well, old chap! we must be going, or we'll miss the train, and that wouldn't do, eh, Cock Robin?"

"One moment, Peter; it all looks so bright, I can't bear to leave it."

"Aye, so it is, and it'll be pleasant to think of afterwards."

"Yes; but, O Peter, it is just like his dying to lose him so! Oh, I wish I could go, too!" and the boy's voice shook with a rising sob.

"What, and leave your work?"

"I could have got work there."

"Not *your own* work, though, which just

now is to cheer up a stupid old chap who feels a bit down, and wants Cock Robin to make him laugh."

"O master, dear old master!" and now Robin's tears were flowing fast, though from a different cause; and even his father was for a time forgotten in his anxiety to atone for the involuntary slight cast on his faithful old friend.

Then master and servant went back to Burnside together, and Robin began the life of simple, honest labour, which he still holds to, though now he is his own master, and has been so since, ten years ago, Peter Barnet laid down the old hammer for ever, and folded the strong hands which had toiled so hard, in rest after the long day's work.

Robin never saw his father again. His intemperate life had left its effects on his health, that could never be effaced even by Martin's tenderest care and attention, and he died in little more than a year after reaching Australia.

But his last days were full of hope—hope in God's mercy, and such earnest struggles

with sin, as come only of faith and hope in
Him who breaks not the bruised reed, nor
quenches the smoking flax. "We cannot
sorrow for his death," wrote Martin to his
brother; "he is only one more gone to our
Home, where we shall all meet again some
day, please God."

And to that Home Robin Hill looks now
more eagerly than ever, for he alone remains
of those of whom this story has been the
history.

Not that it yet seems near, to look at the
hale strong man, as different from the pale,
weakly child we can remember, as is Master
Hill, the prosperous and much respected
blacksmith of Burnside, from little Robin,
the neglected, forsaken little vagabond of
the village.

But still the years pass by quickly, and
Master Hill's dark hair is streaked with
grey; and often amidst his work, in the roar
of the furnace and the song of the anvil, the
thought comes back to him : " Life is good,
and work is good; but the Sabbath day's rest
comes at last."

PUBLICATIONS

OF THE

Society for Promoting Christian Knowledge.

*Most of these Works may be had in ornamental bindings,
with gilt edges, at a small extra charge.*

	Price.	
	s.	d.
A TALE OF TWO BROTHERS. By James F. Cobb, Esq. 18mo., cloth boards	1	6
ALONE AMONG THE ZULUS. By a Plain Woman. The Narrative of a Journey through the Zulu Country, South Africa. Fcap. 8vo., bevelled boards, gilt edges	2	6
ANIMAL CREATION, The; a popular introduction to Zoology. By Thomas Rymer Jones, Esq., Professor of Natural History and Comparative Anatomy in King's College, London. Illustrated with nearly 500 engravings, 12mo., cloth boards . .	7	6
ASTRONOMY WITHOUT MATHEMATICS. By E. B. Denison, Esq., LL.D., Q.C. Fcap. 8vo., cloth boards. New edition, revised and enlarged . . .	3	0
AUSTRALIA; its Physical Features, Inhabitants, Natural History, and Productions, &c., &c., together with an account of its various British Colonies; with map and six full page illustrations. Fcap. 8vo.	3	6
BATTLE WORTH FIGHTING, and other STORIES. Fcap. 8vo., cloth boards	2	0

Price.
s. d.

BIBLE PICTURE BOOK, complete, containing 96 plates, printed in three colors. Cloth boards . . 5 0
In two vols.:—OLD AND NEW TESTAMENT. Limp cloth . . . . each 2 0
BIBLE PICTURES AND STORIES. In two vols. With 96 plates, printed in colors:—OLD AND NEW TESTAMENT. Extra cloth gilt . . each 7 0
BRITISH BIRDS IN THEIR HAUNTS. By the Rev. C. A. Johns 12 0
CARPENTER'S FAMILY, The; a Sketch of Village Life. By Mrs. Joseph Lamb (Ruth Buck). With four full page engravings on toned paper. Crown 8vo., cloth boards 2 0
CHARLEY WATSON, the Drunkard's little Son . . 1 6
CHEMISTRY OF CREATION; a Sketch of the Chief Chemical and Physical Phenomena of the Earth, Air, and Ocean. By Robert Ellis, F.L.S., &c. &c., Fcap. 8vo., cloth boards. New and revised edition 5 0
COLONIAL EMPIRE of GREAT BRITAIN, The; considered chiefly with reference to its Physical Geography and Industrial Productions. In four vols, Fcap. 8vo., cloth boards. Vol. I. . . 1 6
Vol. II. to IV., each 2 0
CONFIRMATION CLASS, The; or, the History of a Year in Three Lives. By a Clergyman's Wife. Addressed to Village Girls. 18mo., cloth boards . 1 6
DEWDROP AND THE MIST. By Charles Tomlinson, Esq. New Edition 3 6
DIFFICULTY HILL, and SOME LADS WHO CLIMBED IT. 18mo., cloth boards 1 6
EARTH'S MANY VOICES. First and Second Series. With Illustrations, on toned paper. Royal 16mo., extra cloth, gilt edges, each 2 0
The two series in one volume 4 0

Price.
s. d.

EDNA WILLIS; or, the Promise Fulfilled. 18mo., cloth
boards 1 0

ELDAD THE PILGRIM; a Sketch of the Manners and
Customs of the Jews in the Century preceding the
Advent of Our Saviour. Fcap. 8vo., cloth boards 3 0

EVENINGS at the MICROSCOPE; or Researches among
the Minuter Organs and Forms of Animal Life.
By P. H. Gosse, F.R.S. Post 8vo., cloth boards . 6 0

FATHER AND DAUGHTER. 18mo., cloth boards . . 1 0

FETCHING AND KEEPING. Ditto   ditto   . . 1 0

FLOWERING PLANTS, GRASSES, AND FERNS OF GREAT
BRITAIN. By Anne Pratt. New Edition. In
four volumes, containing 319 colored plates. Gilt
edges 42 0

FLOWERS of the FIELD. By Rev. C. A. Johns. Sixth
edition. Fcap. 8vo., cloth boards . . . 7 0

FOREST TREES. Two vols. By ditto   ditto   . 7 6

FOREST TREES of BRITAIN. By Rev. C. A. Johns.
Fcap. 8vo., cloth boards 7 0

FOUR SEASONS, The. Containing 40 plates, printed
in colors, with descriptive Poetry. Royal 16mo.,
gilt edges 5 0

GEORGE COX'S REPENTANCE. 18mo., cloth boards . 2 0

GOLD-STONE BROOCH, The.   Ditto   ditto   . 1 0

HEARTHSTONE BOY, The. 18mo., cloth boards . . 1 6

HISTORY of the CRUSADES, with four full page engravings. By G. G. Perry, M.A. Fcap. 8vo.,
cloth boards, gilt edges 2 6

HOW WE DINE; or, "Dinner's Ready." 18mo., cloth
boards 1 6

| | Price. |
| | s. d |

NATURAL HISTORY, Illustrated Sketches of. First
and second series. Fcap. 8vo., cloth boards, each — 2 6

NATURAL HISTORY PRINTS, with Letterpress Descriptions, containing 210 pictures. Half morocco,
cloth sides, gilt edges . . . . plain 42 0

——————————————————colored 68 0

OCEAN, The. By P. H. Gosse, F.R.S. Post 8vo.,
cloth boards 4 6

OLIVE, THE TEACHER. 18mo., cloth boards . . 1 6

OUR NATIVE SONGSTERS. By Anne Pratt. 73 colored
plates. Royal 16mo., cloth boards . . . 8 0

PENNY WISE AND POUND FOOLISH. By Mrs. Carey
Brock. Fcap. 8vo., cloth boards 2 6

PEOPLE OF EUROPE. First and second series in a vol.
24 colored plates. Royal 16mo., limp cloth . . 2 6

PERSEVERANCE UNDER DIFFICULTIES, as shown in
the Lives of Great Men. Fcap. 8vo., cloth boards — 2 6

PHILIP MAVOR; or, Life among the Kaffirs. By W.
H. G. Kingston, Esq. 18mo., cloth boards . . 1 0

PHILLIS; or, the Jealous One 1 6

PICTURES AND STORIES FOR LITTLE CHILDREN. By
Isabella E. Glennie. 18mo., cloth boards . . 1 0

PITCAIRN; with a short Notice of the Original Settlement and present Condition of Norfolk Island.
By the late Rev. T. B. Murray, M.A. Fcap. 8vo.,
cloth boards 2 0

RECOLLECTIONS OF A VISIT TO BRITISH KAFFRARIA.
Fcap. 8vo., cloth boards 2 0

ROBINSON CRUSOE. New Edition. With 4 page
engravings. 12mo., cloth boards 3 0

ROB NIXON, THE OLD WHITE TRAPPER. By W. H.
G. Kingston, Esq. 18mo., cloth boards . . 1 6

ROME AND ITS RUINS, with a Map and eight full page engravings. By W. Forsyth, Esq., Q.C. Fcap. 8vo., cloth boards, gilt edges 2 6

SANDWICH ISLANDS AND THEIR PEOPLE, The. By M. A. Donne, Author of "Denmark and its People," &c. Fcap. 8vo., cloth boards . . . 2 0

SCRIPTURE MANNERS and CUSTOMS. Fcap. 8vo., cloth boards 6 0

SCRIPTURE TOPOGRAPHY. PALESTINE. With Maps. Fcap. 8vo., cloth boards 6 0

SCRIPTURE TOPOGRAPHY. GENTILE WORLD. With Map. Fcap. 8vo., cloth boards 6 0

SCRIPTURE NATURAL HISTORY. Fcap. 8vo., cloth boards 6 0

SELBORNE, NATURAL HISTORY OF. By the late Rev. Gilbert White, A.M. Arranged for Young Persons. A new and revised Edition Post 8vo., cloth boards 5 0

SHIPWRECKS and ADVENTURES at SEA. Fcap. 8vo., cloth boards 2 6

SHORT STORIES FOUNDED ON EUROPEAN HISTORY.— FRANCE, ITALY, SPAIN, SWEDEN, SWITZERLAND, 16mo., each 2 0

SKETCHES of the AFRICAN KINGDOMS and PEOPLES; with a map and numerous illustrations. Fcap. 8vo., cloth boards 4 0

STORIES FOR EVERY SUNDAY IN THE CHRISTIAN YEAR. Fcap. 8vo., cloth boards 2 0

————on "MY DUTY TOWARDS GOD." Crown 8vo., cloth boards . . . . , . 1 6

————on "MY DUTY TOWARDS MY NEIGHBOUR." Crown 8vo., cloth boards 2 0

Price.
s. d.

TOM BARTON'S TRIAL, and other Stories. 18mo., cloth boards 1 0

TOM NEAL AND SARAH HIS WIFE, The EXPERIENCES OF. Crown 8vo., cloth boards 1 6

TOY BOOKS FOR CHILDREN. In an Ornamental Cover. Demy 4to., each containing six large colored plates, with descriptive Letterpress in large type :—

    I.—PRETTY PICTURES OF PRETTY BIRDS . 1 0

    II.—BUTTERCUPS AND DAISIES AND OTHER PRETTY FLOWERS 1 0

TRAVELS BY LAND AND SEA; The Old Arm Chair. Fcap. 8vo., cloth boards 3 0

VICTOR : a Tale of the Great Persecution. Fcap. 8vo., cloth boards, gilt edges 1 6

VICTOR LECZINSKI ; or, the Road to Siberia. 18mo., cloth boards 1 0

WILD FLOWERS. By Ann Pratt. In two vols., containing 192 plates, printed in colors. 16mo., cloth boards 16 0

WINIFRED LEIGH. By the Author of "Harry's Battles," &c. Fcap. 8vo., cloth boards . . 1 6

WINNIE'S DIFFICULTIES; or, "Which are my Duties?" Fcap. 8vo., cloth boards 1 6

WOODBURY FARM. 18mo., cloth boards . . . 1 6

WRECK OF THE OSPREY, The; a Story for Boys. Fcap. 8vo., cloth boards 1 6

YEAR OF COUNTRY LIFE ; or, Chronicle of the Young Naturalists. Fcap. 8vo., cloth boards . . 2 6

NEW COTTAGE WALL PRINTS.

PRINTED IN COLORS,

From Original Drawings by Eminent Artists.

Size 14 by 11 inches.

HAYFIELD,	TRAWLING BY NIGHT.
CORNFIELD,	STORM,
STRAWYARD,	BIRD'S NEST.

Each 6*d*., in glazed frames 1*s*., in gilt frames 2*s*.

Depositories :

77, GREAT QUEEN STREET, LINCOLN'S INN FIELDS;

4, ROYAL EXCHANGE; 48, PICCADILLY

AND BY ALL BOOKSELLERS.

Check Out More Titles From HardPress Classics Series In this collection we are offering thousands of classic and hard to find books. This series spans a vast array of subjects – so you are bound to find something of interest to enjoy reading and learning about.

Subjects:
Architecture
Art
Biography & Autobiography
Body, Mind &Spirit
Children & Young Adult
Dramas
Education
Fiction
History
Language Arts & Disciplines
Law
Literary Collections
Music
Poetry
Psychology
Science
…and many more.

Visit us at www.hardpress.net

Im The Story
personalised classic books

JANE
IN
WONDERLAND

LEWIS
CARROLL

"Beautiful gift... lovely finish.
My Niece loves it, so precious!"

Helen R Brumfieldon

⭐⭐⭐⭐⭐

UNIQUE
GIFT

FOR KIDS, PARTNERS
AND FRIENDS

Timeless books such as:

Kids

Alice in Wonderland · The Jungle Book · The Wonderful Wizard of Oz
Peter and Wendy · Robin Hood · The Prince and The Pauper
The Railway Children · Treasure Island · A Christmas Carol

Adults

Romeo and Juliet · Dracula

Highly Customizable

Change Books Title

Replace Characters Names with yours

Upload Photo for inside pages

Add Inscriptions

Visit
Im The Story .com
and order yours today!